THE WEAPONS ENCYCLOPÆDIA
TANK AIRCRAFT AFV SHIP ARTILLERY VEHICLES SECRET WEAPON

TWE-017 EN

T-26 LIGHT TANK

THE WEAPONS ENCYCLOPAEDIA

EDITORIAL STAFF
Luca Cristini, Paolo Crippa.

ACADEMIC STAFF
Enrico Acerbi, Massimiliano Afiero, Aldo Antonicelli, Ruggero Calò, Luigi Carretta, Flavio Chistè, Anna Cristini, Carlo Cucut, Salvo Fagone, Enrico Finazzer, Arturo Giusti, Björn Huber, Andrea Lombardi, Aymeric Lopez, Marco Lucchetti, Luigi Manes, Giovanni Maressi, Francesco Mattesini, Péter Mujzer, Federico Peirani, Alberto Peruffo, Maurizio Raggi, Andrea Alberto Tallillo, Antonio Tallillo, Massimo Zorza.

PUBLISHED BY
Luca Cristini Editore (Soldiershop), via Orio, 35/4 - 24050 Zanica (BG) ITALY.

DISTRIBUTION BY
Soldiershop - www.soldiershop.com, Amazon, Ingram Spark, Berliner Zinnfigurem (D), LaFeltrinelli, Mondadori, Libera Editorial (Spain), Google book (eBook), Kobo, (eBoook), Apple Book (eBook).

PUBLISHING'S NOTES
None of unpublished images or text of our book may be reproduced in any format without the expressed written permission of Luca Cristini Editore (already Soldiershop.com) when not indicate as marked with license creative commons 3.0 or 4.0. Luca Cristini Editore has made every reasonable effort to locate, contact and acknowledge rights holders and to correctly apply terms and conditions to Content. Every effort has been made to trace the copyright of all the photographs. If there are unintentional omissions, please contact the publisher in writing at: info@soldiershop.com, who will correct all subsequent editions.

LICENSES COMMONS
This book may utilize part of material marked with license creative commons 3.0 or 4.0 (CC BY 4.0), (CC BY-ND 4.0), (CC BY-SA 4.0) or (CC0 1.0). We give appropriate attribution credit and indicate if change were made in the acknowledgments field. Our WTW books series utilize only fonts licensed under the SIL Open Font License or other free use license.

CONTRIBUTORS OF THIS VOLUME & ACKNOWLEDGEMENTS
Ringraziamo i principali collaboratori di questo numero: I profili dei carri sono tutti dell'autore. Le colorazioni delle foto sono di Anna Cristini. Ringraziamenti particolari a istituzioni nazionali e/o private quali: Stato Maggiore dell'esercito, Archivio di Stato, Bundesarchiv, Nara, Library of Congress ecc. A P.Crippa, A.Lopez, L.Manes, C.Cucut, archivi Tallillo. Model Victoria (www.modelvictoria.it), per avere messo a disposizione immagini o altro dei loro archivi.

For a complete list of Soldiershop titles, or for every information please contact us on our website: www.soldiershop.com or www.cristinieditore.com. E-mail: info@soldiershop.com. Keep up to date on Facebook & Twitter: https://www.facebook.com/soldiershop.publishing

Title: **RUSSIAN LIGHT TANK T-26** Code.: **TWE-017 EN**
Series by L. S. Cristini
ISBN code: 9791255890508. First edition December 2023.
THE WEAPONS ENCYCLOPAEDIA (SOLDIERSHOP) is a trademark of Luca Cristini Editore

THE WEAPONS ENCYCLOPÆDIA
TANK AIRCRAFT AFV SHIP ARTILLERY VEHICLES SECRET WEAPON

RUSSIAN LIGHT TANK T-26

LUCA STEFANO CRISTINI

BOOK SERIES FOR MODELERS & COLLECTORS

CONTENTS

Introduction 5
   - Development and design 6
   - Technical features 8

Main variants and derivatives 11
   - Variants of T-26 11
   - Derived vehicles 14
   - Other vehicles mounted on the T-26 *chassis* 18

Operational use 23
   - Spain: the baptism of fire 23
   - The unknown border war against Japan 29
   - The Winter War against Finland 30
   - The Great Patriotic War 30
   - Last fires 33
   - Conclusion 35

Production and export 47
Data sheet 52
Bibliography 58

INTRODUCTION

The T-26 is a Soviet light tank used for infantry support, based on the British Vickers Mk E tank, adopted by the USSR in 1931 with the regular purchase of the British licence.
It was by far the highest-producing tank of the Red Army and the Finnish Army at the beginning of World War II, as well as of the Army of the Spanish Republic during the Spanish Civil War, the second largest after the legendary Soviet T-34 tank of the 1930s and 1940s. It was not, therefore, an autonomous project, as for practical and strategic reasons the USSR needed to gain lost ground in industrial production.
In the early 1930s, the bulk of the USSR's tanks consisted mainly of the T-18 light tank, mass-produced for direct infantry support, and various types of British tanks from the First World War. The T-18 fulfilled the task of saturating the Red Army with combat-ready and relatively modern tanks, as well as their development by industry. However, the characteristics of the T-18 never fully seduced the Red Army General Staff. At a council meeting at the end of 1929, it was concluded that, due to the lack of experience among Soviet tank designers and the underdeveloped industrial base, it was advisable to turn to selected foreign models. In May 1930, a contract was then signed for 15 Vickers 6-tonne Model A (double turret) vehicles, with full documentation and plans for domestic production. The 15 tanks were assembled in 1930 at Vickers, under the careful care of Soviet engineers. The first vehicles arrived in the USSR in the autumn of that year and the others in 1931-32, when the first national T-26 design was almost ready for production.

◀ ▲ A perfect example of an early model T-26 with two twin turrets armed with 7.62 mm BT machine guns, preserved at the Australian armour and artillery museum. CC3.

DEVELOPMENT AND DESIGN

The first T-26 tanks, which were derived directly from the Vickers model, had appeared in 1931 and were armed with two parallel turrets, in the centre of the hull, equipped with a light machine gun on each turret. The three-place version was not sufficiently armed; it was then decided to upgrade the weapon system by replacing a light machine gun with a heavy one in the T-26 A-3. This intermediate solution did not last long and, after replacing the heavy machine gun with a 27 mm cannon (T-26A-4) or 37 mm cannon (T-26A-5), the most modern solution was finally arrived at, i.e. switching from a multiple turret to a single turret in the T-26B-1 version equipped with a 37 mm cannon; thus moving from two single-seat turrets to a two-seat one, although this prevented the engagement of two targets at once, which was important for a slow vehicle like the T-26 infantry support vehicle. But the solution soon proved to be the best.

Next, the 37-mm cannon derived from the 3.7-cm PaK 36 produced by Rheinmetall was replaced by a 45-mm cannon with a 46-calibre barrel (L/46). This increased the armour-piercing but above all explosive power (1.4 kg grenade at 700ms) even further. This successful model went down in history as the *Model 1933* (the previous T-26A in its various declinations was known as the *Model 1931*), and was produced, on its own, in about 5,500 examples, thus half of all T-26s produced! It should also be noted that this production was achieved in just three years, an exceptional production rate for the time.

The T-26 underwent further evolutions, then the *T-26S Model 1937* appeared, equipped, like the last examples of the Model 1933, with welded instead of riveted type armour. This choice was due to the fact that the type of rivet adopted often ended up as a sort of projectile against the tank crew if hit. Other derivative versions of the T-26 were the *OT-26* flamethrower with a flamethrower instead of a cannon, the *OT-33* which had both, the ST-26 bridge crane to give the tank units the necessary mobility against natural obstacles, and the *T-26A-4(U)* and *T-26B-2(U)* command tank, equipped with a railing radio. Other attempts were for a self-propelled tank with a 76 mm M1927 cannon.

▲ T-26 tank still of the first type with double turret, but with two different weapon systems. A new 37 gun on the right turret and the usual 7.62 DT gun on the other turret. Model preserved at the Patriotic Museum in Kuninka, Russia.

T-26 LIGHT TANK MOD. 1931 KHALKIN GOL, AUGUST 1939

▲ T-26 A1 twin turret version with two 7.62 mm DT machine guns.

TECHNICAL FEATURES

The T-26 was to all intents and purposes a light tank, designed expressly for troop support, and consequently was not particularly well endowed in terms of mobility, with an engine and transmission of modest overall power, giving a relatively low speed.

The armour plating was flat sheet metal, at least in the 1933/T-26B model, the most common and best-known tank in this family. The internal structure was very similar to that of a conventional type vehicle: pilot forward, tank leader and gunner in the turret. The latter, of cylindrical or rectangular structure, was shifted significantly to the left of the hull. There was no space for a loader, but even with a two-man crew, the ergonomics were acceptable, as was the interior volume.

The engine was positioned at the rear and transmitted motion to the front wheels via a drive shaft. The two engine fans were protected by ventilation grilles at the rear of the engine bonnet. The 45 mm long 46-calibre cannon was an effective weapon, capable of prevailing over any tank of the time, with a useful range of over 1,000 metres. Having twice the mass of a 37mm shell, it also had much more explosive power, making it a multi-purpose weapon. Two machine guns, one in front and one aimed at the rear of the tower, were present as auxiliary armaments. The two crewmen had upper hatches on the turret, but also two periscopes for observation and aiming, although there was no dome for the tank leader.

▲ ▶ Interior of the turret of the T-26 tank model 1933. This is a model captured by the Finnish Armed Forces and exhibited in the Finnish Tank Museum (Panssarimuseo) in Parola. This particular tank has been restored to make it drivable. Wiki CC3.

The armour was riveted, but the later types, as it turned out, had a more reliable welded armour, which gave better strength for the same weight. The tank structure did not use the advantage of the inclined planes to increase resistance to enemy fire, presenting large vertical parts. The steel used was of excellent quality and greatly enhanced thicknesses, although these were only intended to counter the threat of shrapnel and light projectiles.

Mobility was not exceptional, but it was better than that of many infantry tanks on the road, but in overcoming obstacles and ditches the vehicle showed some difficulty (0.80 metres and 1.90 metres respectively). The rolling train, powered by a petrol engine, consisted of metal tracks with a front wheel, a rear wheel, 3 track rollers and 4 bogies with 2 track rollers on each side.

Double turret models

The first manufactured models of the Soviet T-26 were still of the archaic double turret type. Each turret had its own observation slot, a round firing port for the DT machine gun, armoured plates riveted to the frame and even sealed zinc shims to improve river and stream fording performance. A cover was later added for the engine's main air outlet window. The models built in 1932-33 had a mixed construction, with a welded and riveted hull. The two turrets were riveted or welded, mounted on hulls that were themselves welded or riveted. These turrets were made in four different designs and configurations, but always assembled in the same position. Each individual turret had an arc of fire of 240° and armour of between 13 and 15 mm, greatly improving on the precarious armouring of the early models, which had only 10 mm of alloy, among other things shoddy, which struggled to block enemy machine-gun bullets. The first models were produced in the following runs: the 1931 model in 100 examples, the 1932 around 1350 examples, and finally the 1933 around 580 examples; they were all double turret versions. In all, just over 2,000 were built. Their combat value in 1939 was already insignificant, so many were converted to other tasks and some to training.

The most successful single turret and new turret model: the Mod. 1938

However, the double turret was short-lived and production was limited: major production took off with the single turret T-26. This time it was completely Soviet designed. The turret was cylindrical, relatively low, simple in design, with rear storage, and housed a 45mm cannon with decent anti-tank capabilities. This was a very positive change from the 37 mm cannon of the 'British' Type B version. Then from 1933 to 1938, the T-26 underwent few changes, except for the use of more modern whip antennas, the VKU-3 control system, the TPU-3 intercom, and an electric shutter and vertically stabilised telescopic sight.

The main armament remained unchanged until the end of production, which was in 1941 due to obvious unsuitability in comparison to the new enemy tanks, but the 1938 model received a brand new cast turret with slanted angles, the same armour and an improved panoramic sight for the command tanks with radio system.

This turret was also prepared for a rear gun sight, first introduced in 1935, for a third DT machine gun. After the summer of 1938, the turret base was reinforced and provided with an improved armour thickness of 20 mm. This last model was christened the 1939 model. In total, 4,826 tanks of the 1938 and 1939 models were built; about 670 of these were equipped with anti-aircraft machine gun mounts in 1939-40. At the same time, several old obsolete models were converted into flamethrowers or special tanks for chemical battalions. In 1940, the S. Kirov automobile factory in Leningrad was commissioned to modernise 340 old and obsolete 1933 T-26 models. These were subjected to many changes such as increased armour for the headlights, addition of a side door for the driver and the installation of new armoured observation devices, a common hatch above the engine compartment and new access to the fuel tank, which was also made more capable.

▲ Very clear detail of the shape of the front hatch for the turret driver of the T-26 tank model 1933. Finnish version of the Finnish Tank Museum (Panssarimuseum) in Parola. Wiki CC3.

MAIN VARIANTS AND DERIVATIVES

■ **VARIANTS OF THE T-26**

The Soviet T-26 was an important tank, although not too strategic, given that we are talking about a light vehicle. It was, as mentioned, produced in more than 10,000 units (and almost 12,000, considering the vehicles derived from or mounted on the T-26 *chassis*); quite a lot, which meant that the Russians believed in it. The basic model, the one used as a light tank in infantry support, was divided into 6 models, indicated by the year, namely: model 1931, 1932, 1933, 1937, 1938 and 1939. These 5 models were produced for an entire decade, from 1931 to 1941. This vehicle had already had its day during the Nazi invasion of the USSR, but the experience served the Soviets well in organising mass production of armoured vehicles and mastering good technologies, such as high quality armour, high speed guns and on-board radios.

THE 1931 MODEL

The **T-26 model 1931 was the** first line tank, in the basic two-tower version with cannon-machine gun armament (37 mm cannon in one of the towers and machine gun in the other).

THE 1932 MODEL

The **1932 model,** like the previous line tank, was still based on the two-tower version with armament by two 7.62 BT machine guns. In all, some 2038 of the Model 1932 were built. Their combat value in 1939 was insignificant, so many were converted to other tasks and some to training. This was the last model designed with two turrets.

THE 1933 MODEL

The **T-26 model 1933** - line tank, was the first with the single turret version of the cylindrical type and 45 mm cannon, the most popular option. In what was to become the most popular model produced in over 5,000 units.

▲ T-26 early production version (1932 model) undergoing maintenance in a Russian barracks. Wiki CC3.

THE 1936 MODEL

The monumental Model 1933 was followed by the **Model 1936** - an experimental machine with a 37 mm Boris Shpitalny automatic anti-aircraft gun installed in the turret. Due to the unreliability of the cannon, work on the creation of an anti-aircraft tank was soon halted.

THE 1938 AND 1939 MODELS

The last two models, the 1938 and 1939 line tanks, were fitted with a new, more modern single conical turret and welded hull. The conical turret was also again revised with further improvements and new sloping walls. These last two versions of the T-26 were also produced in large numbers, around 4,850 or slightly less. Many of these were equipped with anti-aircraft support with a machine gun mounted on the turret top. The story of the T-26 did not end there, however, as from its 'ashes' (for the models judged to be no longer for combat use), a company specially set up in Leningrad (but it was not the only one) was responsible for the creation of several variants, for different uses and for a few dozen models that we will analyse later.

Next we will illustrate other different variants of the T-26 tank, designed for various missions: command-radio tanks, with teletank modules (telemechanical group), with an artillery support function, flamethrower versions, and genius versions. And again, artillery tractors, electric tanks and more. We will complete with a third section dedicated to vehicles on T-26 chassis.

▲ T-26 tank model 1933. This is still the model captured by the Finnish Armed Forces, and repainted and reassigned by them with the titular *runich* insignia, a kind of Finnish swastika. The tank is on display in the Finnish Tank Museum (Panssarimuseo) in Parola. Wiki CC3.

T-26RT LIGHT TANK MOD. 1933 MOSCOW PARADE, MAY 1935

THE DERIVATIVES OF T-26

- **T-26RT:** single turret tank with radio station 71-TK-1 (from 1933);

- **TU-26 / TT-26:** tank and *teletank of the* first series of the telemechanical group, also known as remote-controlled. They were equipped with TOZ-6 equipment and built on the chassis of the linear T-26. In 1936-37, 35 vehicle groups of each type were converted from 2-turret tanks to single-turret versions;

- **TU-132 / TT-131:** control and *teletank* (TT) tank of the second series of the telemechanical group. They were equipped with TOZ-8 equipment. The TT-131s were built on the basis of the XT-130s. In 1938-39, 30 groups were formed. 55 tanks were built from scratch in 1938 and 5 were converted from 2 turrets in 1939;

- **T-26A:** artillery support tank. A new, more spacious T-26-4 turret with a 76 mm short-barrelled gun was installed. Six prototypes were produced.

Flame-throwing tanks made up about 12 per cent of the T-26 series production. These tanks were referred to as 'KhT' (*Khimicheskiy Tank*, 'chemical tank') or XT in contemporary documents. In addition to the use of the flamethrower, these vehicles were also intended for the dispersion of chemical agents and smoke curtains using the TKhP-3 equipment, developed in 1932 and easily installed on all T-26 tanks;

- **XT-26:** flamethrower tank. The armament was located in a small turret. 552 tanks were produced and 53 were converted from the standard T-26 to two turrets;

- **XT-130:** flamethrower tank, variant of the 1933 model year; the flamethrower is mounted in a cylindrical turret instead of a cannon. 401 vehicles were produced;

- **XT-133:** flamethrower tank, a variant of the 1938 model year, with the flamethrower mounted in a conical turret. 269 tanks produced;

- **XT-134:** flamethrower tank, variant of the 1939 model. Armament: 45 mm 20K cannon model 1932/38, flamethrower in the hull, 2 DT machine guns, two prototypes converted from T-26 linear.

▲ One of the various flamethrower versions made from the T-26, called XT. Over a thousand of the four different versions XT 26, 130, 133 and 134 were made. The one pictured is still the first model. This vehicle was produced in 1935 and partially modernised between 1938 and 1940.

T-26 LIGHT TANK MOD. 1931 KHALKIN GOL, AUGUST 1939

▲ T-26 A1 command tank radio version with twin turrets with a 37mm cannon and a 7.62mm DT machine gun.

- **ST-26:** engineer tank (bridge caster) (1932-1939). Armament: DT machine gun, 65 vehicles produced and converted into 6 experimental tanks of different systems. The special equipment consisted of a 7.35 m long metal deck weighing 1,100 kg. The ST-26 was designed to enable the T-27, T-26 and BT tanks to cross trenches and ditches 6-6.5 m wide;
- **T-263:** light tank with electric drive (1935-1938). Armament: 45 mm cannon model 1932 and 2 DT machine guns. Only one prototype was produced;
- **KT-26:** tracked wheeled light tank.

▲ ST-26 pioneer tank with bridge-casting system during trials in March 1933. In the small photos: top: AT-1 armed with 76.2 mm PS-3 tank gun. Below: SU-5-1 self-propelled vehicle armed with 76 mm divisional cannon.

T-26 LIGHT TANK MOD. 1931/32, RUSSIA 1939

▲ T-26 A1 tank version with cannon and machine gun armament - two-sided version with 37 mm Hotchkiss gun (PS-1) in the right turret.

OTHER VEHICLES MOUNTED ON THE T-26 CHASSIS

Self-propelled artillery vehicles: vehicles built on the *chassis* of the T-26 and used in the field of self-propelled artillery direct or mock transport or tractor.

- **SU-5-1**: self-propelled artillery vehicle armed with the 76 mm M1902/30 divisional gun, with an open fighting compartment. A single prototype built in 1934;

- **SU-5-2**: self-propelled artillery vehicle armed with the 122 mm M1910/30 howitzer, with open fighting compartment. A prototype built in 1934, followed by 30 production vehicles in 193;

- **SU-5-3**: self-propelled artillery vehicle armed with the 152 mm divisional howitzer M1931 (NM), with an open fighting compartment. A prototype built in 1934;

- **SU-6**: self-propelled anti-aircraft gun armed with 76.2 mm 3K anti-aircraft gun, with open combat compartment. A prototype built in 1935. It was planned to produce four production vehicles in 1936, equipped with 37 mm ZSU-37s;

-**SU-T-26** (**SU-26**, later **SU-76P**): anti-aircraft self-propelled vehicle with an open combat compartment, armed with ZSU-37 anti-aircraft machine gun or 76 mm M1927 divisional cannon. The Kirov Factory in Leningrad built 14 vehicles in 1941: 2 with 37 mm machine guns and 12 with 76 mm cannon;

- **T-26-T**: armoured artillery tractor based on the T-26 chassis. The first version had an unarmoured superstructure, while the T-26-T2 was fully armoured. A small number of tractors were produced in 1933 for motorised artillery batteries towing 76 mm divisional guns. Some of them remained in service until 1945. In 1933, 183 T-26T tractors were produced. Later in 1936, 14 tractors with an upgraded engine and improved towing system were produced, 10 of them with an armoured cab. Field tests and service at the front showed that the vehicle was underpowered for off-road towing of loads greater than 5 t, so the vehicles were not further developed. In May 1941, old double-turret tanks were surrendered, unarmed, by the eastern armoured units to be converted into tractors for regimental and anti-tank pieces of the mechanised army corps.

▲ Test runs of the first M11 medium tank made in Piedmont in 1939.

T-26 A2 LIGHT TANK MOD. 1933 RUSSIA, WINTER 1939

▲ T-26 A2 tank painted white during the Winter War in Finland, unit unknown, Karelian Isthmus, December 1939.

- **TN-26 (Observer):** experimental observation version of the T-26-T, with a radio station and a crew of five;
- **T-26E:** in the Finnish Army, after the Finnish campaign in 1940, Vickers Mk E tanks, rearmed with a Soviet 45 mm cannon, were called T-26E. They were used in 1941-1944 and some remained in service until 1959;
- **TR-1:** troop transport vehicle. Prototype built in early 1933. The 90 hp Hercules engine and transmission were moved to the front of the vehicle. A rear armoured cab carried the infantrymen, equipped with a rear door and 6 side slits. The vehicle was unarmed. Tested between August and October 1933 in Kubinka. *Specifications*: weight: 9.455 t - crew: 2 (tank leader and pilot) + 14 infantrymen;
- **TR-4:** armoured personnel carrier;
- **TR-26:** armoured personnel carrier;
- **TP4-1:** ammunition transporter;
- **TV-26:** ammunition transporter;
- **T-26Ts:** fuel transporter;
- **TTs-26:** fuel transporter.

Reconnaissance vehicles

TN ('TN' stands for *tank nabljudenija* or 'observation tank'): an experimental version of an observation tank based on the hull of the T-26T artillery tractor and intended for front-line reconnaissance and observation of artillery fire. Developed by the Moscow Military Supply Depot design office in September 1934. A single vehicle was built and successfully tested in 1935. The TN had an armoured casemate instead of a turret, armed with a DT machine gun. The special equipment consisted of a 71-TK-1 radio station with a handrail antenna around the cab, a Zeiss optical rangefinder (with a 500 mm base), a PTK panoramic optic for the foreman, a gyrocompass, goniometer, blind spot calculator, predictor, map table, SPVO traffic light telegraph and two UNAF telephones with wire nosepiece. *Specifications*: weight: 8.1 t - crew: 3 - armour: 6-15 mm - speed: 28 km/h - range: 130 km.

▲ A rare image of the TR-1 troop transport vehicle.

T-26 A2 LIGHT TANK MOD. 1936/37 RUSSIA, WINTER 1939

▲ T-26 A2 command tank, with the characteristic radio antenna on the handrail, additional twin headlights, DT P40 anti-aircraft mount and DT mount on the rear turret. Unknown unit - Mongolian Frontier, August 1939.

BSNP: the TN, in storage at Factory No. 185, was rebuilt as a BSNP (*bronirovannij samochodnij nabljudatel'nij punkt* - 'self-propelled armoured observation post') in 1939. It was equipped with a 71-TK radio station, an Invert optical rangefinder (with a 700-mm base), PTK panoramic optics for the tank leader, a magnetic compass, a retractable periscope for PDN long-distance observation (10× magnification and 5° field), two field telephones with two cable hawsers and a goniometer developed by Research Institute No. 22. The vehicle was tested in the summer of 1939 and the inspection commission came to the conclusion that the BSNP was a very useful vehicle for observing artillery firing and for coordination between artillery, tanks and infantry on the battlefield, but the quality of the equipment and its installation did not allow for optimal use of the vehicle. An improvement of the vehicle was therefore recommended, but all work was stopped;

T-26FT ('FR' stands for photo tank or 'photographic tank'): an experimental reconnaissance vehicle based on the T-26 Mod. 1933, intended to film and photograph enemy defensive works, both stationary and in motion. The T-26FT retained the normal cylindrical turret, with a handrail radio antenna, but the 45 mm cannon was replaced by a wooden simulacrum. Armament was limited to a DT machine gun with 441 rounds on board. On the left side of the turret were two small 80 mm diameter loopholes, equipped with lenses and electrically operated armoured hatches. Inside the vehicle were two special compartments: one was for photographic and film shooting, equipped with a Kinamo heavy semi-automatic camera, a film camera, a periscope synchronised with both of the above and a radio station; the other compartment was for photographic development and was equipped with an Anschütz gyrocompass and an apparatus for enlarging and developing film. The crew consisted of three men: a pilot and two photo-cinematographic operators. A single vehicle was built in 1937 and tested at Kubinka in January-February 1938. No operational developments followed.

▲ BSNP reconnaissance tank. Note the handrail radio antenna and the two windows for the optical rangefinder on the front plate of the hull, July 1941. Small photo: SU-5-3 artillery unit, armed with 152.4 mm Howitzer.

OPERATIONAL USE

The T-26 participated, and was heavily engaged, in numerous battles and campaigns between 1936 and 1942. Its real baptism of fire came in the Spanish Civil War, and was very relevant against the clearly inferior CV33 and Panzer I nationalist tanks, armed only with light machine guns. The Soviet tank could also compete with the more massive Panzer II, and had an effective cannon well over a kilometre. Although the T-26s had quality armour, they were still too light to withstand field and counter-tank artillery, which often put them out of action. Against Japan, the USSR employed these vehicles heavily, and thanks to them won the Battle of Khalkhin Gol under Žukov's command. In this undeclared war in the summer of 1939, the Soviets defeated the Japanese, inflicting far more damage on the enemy than casualties. It was a true Blitzkrieg, the first of the modern tank era, and it was unfortunate that not enough was known in the West about Soviet operational capabilities, which proved to be exemplary. But against Finland first, and much more so during the clash with Germany, from Barbarossa onwards, the vehicle revealed the full extent of its differential, which made the already brilliant T-26s obsolete in a very short time.

SPAIN: THE BAPTISM OF FIRE

The young Soviet armoured levies spent the entire first part of the 1930s training with BTs and T-26s, which then made up the bulk of the Soviet armoured force. The outbreak of the Spanish Civil War offered a chance for their tanks to test what they were worth. The ruling Spain was the 'natural ally' of communist and revolutionary Russia during the Civil War. Spanish power was in the hands of the

▲ A crowd of Spanish citizens in Cordova look at this Soviet T-26 that had just been captured by the Nationalist forces from the Republican forces, and exhibited as a prey of war on Christmas night 1936.

socialist-dominated Republican Party, and they had to contend with the Francoist insurgents, supported by fascist Italy and Nazi Germany. The Soviets sold them, at favourable prices, a total of 281 T-26 tanks (297 according to other sources), starting in October 1936, together with a dozen BT-5s and several hundred armoured cars. From the very first battles, the T-26 proved to be clearly superior to the bizarre array of antiquated vehicles and tanks acquired by the Nationalist insurgents. The tanks deployed by the Nationalists ranged, in fact, from the semi- harmless Italian tankettes (the famous light tanks also known as sardine cans) to the Germans' small and modest Panzer I.

With the exception of an ever-present air threat, a real ace in the hands of the Nationalists, the T-26 dominated the battlefield and raised not a few concerns among the German tank specialists. During the all-Italian battle of Guadalajara (March 1937), the Republican T-26s completely eradicated the armoured opposition (mostly Italian CV-33s). It was a resounding victory, but it was also the last for the 'Rojos'.

▲ Above: Nationalist phalangists observe a captured T-26. Below: two Republican T-26s in the streets of Belcite.

T-26 LIGHT TANK MOD. 1933, SPAIN 1936

▲ Beautiful image of a T-26 of the Republican forces loaded with militiamen armed with rifles.
▼ A beautiful specimen preserved in Spain of the T-26 with the titpic yellow and red coloured turret.

T-26 A2 LIGHT TANK MOD. 1936/37 RUSSIA, WINTER 1941

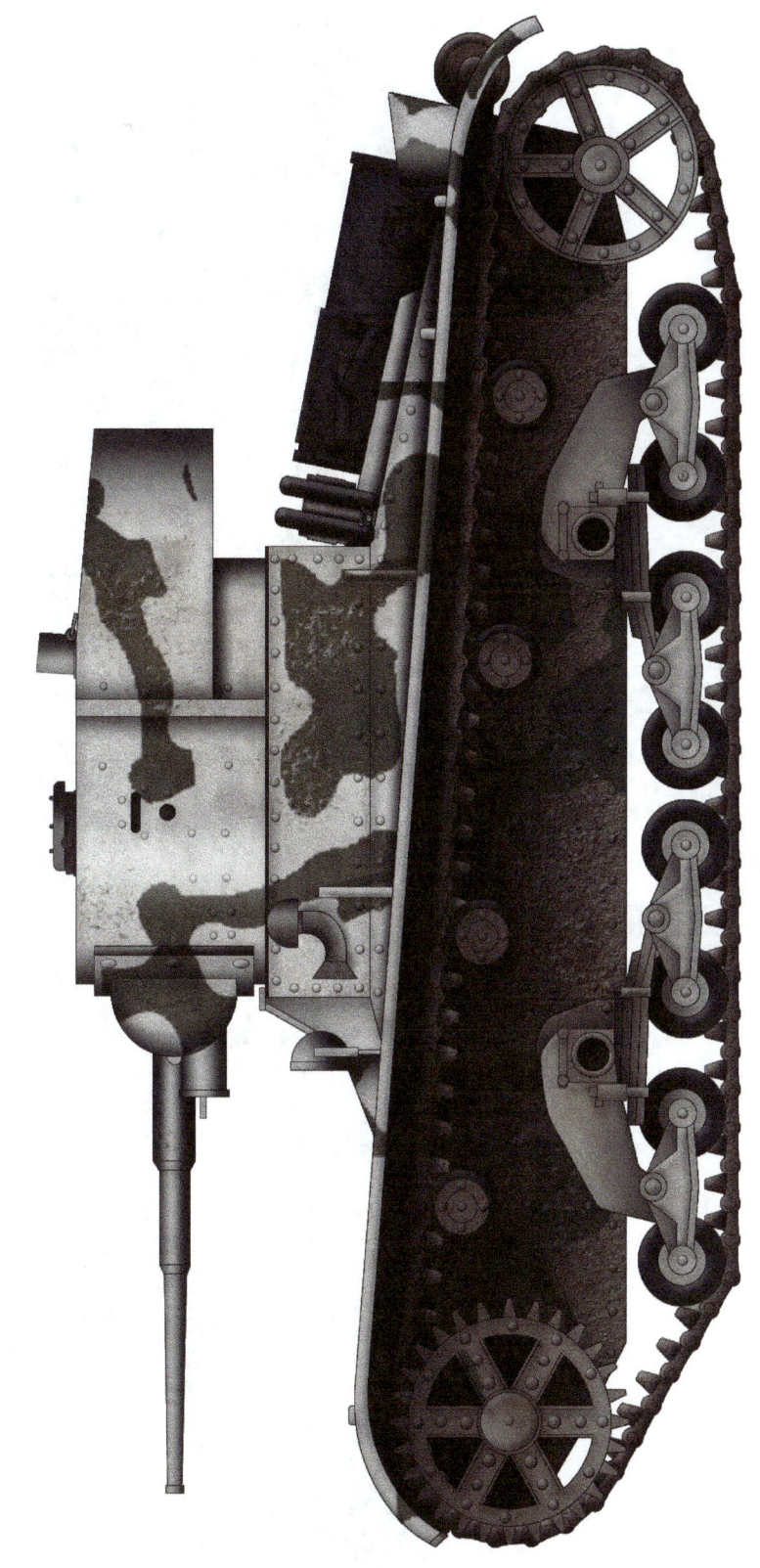

▲ T-26 A2 tank belonging to the 20th Tank Brigade. Russian front, November 1941.

XT-130 FLAME THROWING TANK RUSSIAN-FINNISH WAR, WINTER 1940

▲ XT-130 flamethrower tank, 7th Army Chemical Tank Battalion - Karelian Isthmus, February 1940.

THE UNKNOWN BORDER WAR AGAINST JAPAN

Even before they went to war with Japan in World War II, Russia and Japan had already come to blows. In 1935, the Soviets had recaptured the Tsarist territories in the Far East.

The new borders of the USSR, now recaptured by full force, included the Korean, Chinese and Mongolian borders. Northeast China and its indistinct and ill-defined borders, also due to a desolate, remote and icy geography, had been a source of vivid tensions between Moscow, Beijing and Tokyo since 1905. The area crossed by the Southern Manchuria railway became in particular the *casus belli* that triggered the Second Sino-Japanese War, as well as hundreds of other 'border incidents' (ranging from simple infantry skirmishes to full-scale battles) fought between Mongolian or Soviet forces against the Imperial Japanese Army. The first major clash was the Changkufeng Incident, which occurred on Lake Khasan in July-August 1938, next to the disputed Changkufeng Heights near Korea. The 2ª Mechanized Brigade, the 32nd and 40th Separate Tank Battalions went into action with their 276 tanks, pulling off a crushing Russian victory against a Japanese army that had never excelled in armoured weaponry. This was the prelude to the final, decisive Battle of Nomonanh (Khalkin Gol) in 1939, which ended, however, with a status quo that still did not guarantee great territorial gains for the USSR.

▲ Another nice picture of a Spanish T-26 (probably a nationalist crew ready for the final parade in Madrid). Note the Soviet leather helmets of the tank crew.

THE WINTER WAR AGAINST FINLAND

World War II is approaching. In the West, the controversial, complicated and difficult non-aggression pact between Hitler and Stalin mainly served to buy them more time to strengthen and prepare their armies, all to the mortal detriment of their hated neighbour, Poland. Most of the Soviet armoured forces that participated in Operation Pincer against the Poles consisted of T-26 light tank brigades.

Three months later, those same units formed the weight of an even stronger invasion force on Finland's south-eastern frontier (the famous Karelia Isthmus). The infamous flame-throwing versions were used en masse against the Mannerheim Line in particular. However, the Finns, thanks to their perfect knowledge of the terrain, and especially thanks to excellent anti-tank guns and clever ad hoc infantry tactics, massacred, literally, swarms of T-26s and proved that this model had finally reached a state of obsolescence. In the Soviet Union, this shock triggered an acceleration in tank design towards the next generation in the 1940s.

As a reward for their resistance, the Finns captured around two hundred T-26s of all versions, which were refurbished and returned to service with their swastika in 1941 against their former owners. Some Finnish T-26s were still in active service in 1960.

THE GREAT PATRIOTIC WAR

By June 1941, the Red Army had a huge number of tanks, and as many as 10,268 T-26 tanks of all models and variants. The last one produced, a T-26 model 1939, had just left the factory in February. But despite

▲ T-26 modified with the first BT-5 turret, model often confused with the 'T-26 mod. 1933'. Exhibited at the Tank Museum in Parola, Finland.

SELF-PROPELLED TANK - RUSSO-FINNISH WAR, WINTER 1939

▲ Self-propelled tank (prototype) 40th Light Brigade, 7th Soviet Army - Karelia Isthmus Finland, February 1939.

T-26 A2 LIGHT TANK MOD. 1934 RUSSIA, AUTUMN 1941

▲ T-26 A2 mod. 1934 in force at the Kiev operational district south-west front. August-September 1941.

its moderate modernisation, the T-26 was feeling its age, and Finland had taught us that modern warfare retires vehicles with a speed unthinkable only a decade earlier. The bodywork of its ancestor, the British Mark E, was designed in 1928.

They constituted by far the majority of every mechanised corps in the border military districts, but despite a clear superiority over the German Panzer I and a certain parity with the Czech-built Panzer 35(t) and 38(t) deployed by the Wehrmacht, the T-26s were certainly no match for the 50 mm and 75 mm guns of the Panzer III and IV that formed the main part of every Panzer division.

Their relatively thin armour could withstand Pak 36 fire, but absolutely not any German anti-tank guns. The outcome was thus widely expected. During the initial phase of Operation Barbarossa, the Soviets lost thousands of T-26s, and not only because of enemy action. The emotional shock was tremendous, and the rapid and unstoppable German advance created large pockets, the delicacies of the T-26s showing all their limitations when subjected to close stress. Many broke down or were immobilised due to a lack of spare parts, fuel and poor maintenance. The Luftwaffe's hammering did the rest. By December 1941, perhaps less than a third of the 10,000 T-26s of all types in the USSR remained safe in the eastern sectors and the Far East. The remaining few fought in Moscow, Stalingrad, the Crimea, the Caucasus and the Northern Front (around Leningrad) until the end of 1944.

Moreover, the latest models were very modern for the times. Those still numerous, operating in the Far East ended up participating in the final attack on Manchukuò in August 1945, the last major offensive action of the war, against the Kwantung Army.

■ LAST FIRES

A number of T-26s, part of the 82 sold to the Chinese Nationalist forces in 1938-42, after opposing the Imperial Japanese forces and playing a significant role in the Battle of the Kunlun Pass, fought against the Communists in 1946-47 and remained operational until the early 1950s.

▲ Beautiful picture of a T-26 with a handrail antenna on display in a Russian museum.

▲ View of the Soviet T-26 light tank from above.

CONCLUSION

The T-26 was a tank with articulated characteristics, which allowed it to last a long time, and in some sectors of the front, still active at the end of the conflict. It began its career with honour in the Spanish Civil War, where it was in fact unrivalled. It was also the tank of records: it was produced in greater numbers than any other tank of the period, with over 12,000 units produced, including variants. During the 1930s, the USSR developed no less than 53 variants of the T-26. These included: flame-throwing tanks, combat vehicles, remotely controlled tanks, self-propelled guns, artillery tractors and self-propelled vehicles. 23 of these variants were mass-produced, others were experimental models and remained at prototype level. It was also, for better or worse, the iconic tank in two wars: Spain and Finland.

Declared essentially obsolete at the beginning of World War II, the T-26 was still the most heavily deployed at the start of Operation Barbarossa in 1941. Although in the end two-thirds of them were actually sacrificed in an attempt to curb the offensive. The T-26 fought the Germans and their allies during the Battle of Moscow in 1941-42, the Battle of Stalingrad and the Battle of the Caucasus in 1942-1943; some tank units of the Leningrad Front used their T-26s until 1944. The last use of Soviet T-26 light tanks was in August 1945, during the defeat of the Japanese Kwantung Army in Manchuria.

The T-26 was also a lucky model, being exported and used extensively by Spain, China and Turkey, and even Afghanistan. Many captured vehicles were redeployed in various capacities by the Finnish, German, Romanian and Hungarian armies. As long as it proved useful, the main asset of the vehicle was that it was a reliable and easy-to-maintain tank, and its design was continuously kept alive between 1931 and 1941. No new models of the T-26 were developed after 1940.

▲ A T-26 reintegrated into the Finnish army, to which typical awards and insignia were applied.

▲ Company' photo of a newly produced T-26 from the Soviet workshops, here in the version with a handrail antenna placed along the turret profile.

▼ Hungarian soldiers from the Eastern Front all crowded on and around the T-26 tank. Péter Mujzer Archive.

T-26 A2 MOD. 1933 LIGHT TANK RUSSIA, CRIMEA, MARCH 1942

▲ T-26 A2 mod. 1933 belonging to the 24th Separate Tank Regiment. Crimean Front, March 1942.

▲ View of the Soviet T-26 light tank from the front and back.

T-26 A2 LIGHT TANK MOD. 1933 RUSSIA, AUGUST 1941

▲ T-26 A2 mod. 1933 belonging to the 39th Armoured Division of the 16th Mechanized Corps. Russia, Uman area, August 1941.

T-26 LIGHT TANK

T-26 A2 LIGHT TANK MOD. 1938 FINLAND, FEBRUARY 1940

▲ T-26 A2 mod. 1938 belonging to the 40th Light Tank Brigade, Karelia Istimia, Finland, February 1940.

T-26 A2 LIGHT TANK MOD. 1938, RUSSIA 1941

▲ T-26 A2 mod. 1938 new three-colour camouflage version, Russia 1941.

▲ T-26-mod-1931 with a distinctive turret equipped with a 43mm cannon, also clearly visible is the machine gun on the left. Note also the open condenser hatch. Leningrad 1933.

▼ A T-26 tank engaged in testing. Péter Mujzer Archive.

T-26 LIGHT TANK A2 MOD. 1938 RUSSIA, SUMMER 1941

▲ T-26 tanks in camouflage and inveranal theatre of war, Karelian Isthmus, Finland 1940.

◀ T-26 tank captured by the Finns during the Winter War against the Soviets 1940.

▼ Prototype of the T-26 in the factory observation post version 185 named after Kirov, Leningrad 1935.

T-26 LIGHT TANK A2 MOD. 1938 BELARUS. JUNE 1941

▲ T-26 A2 mod. 1938 belonging to the 18th Division of the 7th Mechanised Corps, Belarus, June 1941.

T-26 A2 LIGHT TANK MOD. 1938 RUSSIA, WINTER 1941-1942

▲ T-26 A2 mod. 1938 with new winter camouflage with grille. Central front Moscow battle, winter 1941-42.

PRODUCTION AND EXPORT

Production of the Soviet light tank dates back to the early 1930s. This ended with the last examples sent onto the assembly line in 1941 (including all derivatives). It was one of the most produced of all Russian vehicles, second only to the fearsome T-34, we are talking about 10,300 units! It was therefore also a rather successful vehicle, used mainly by Soviet Russia, but also by many other nations mentioned below:

- Republican and Nationalist Spain: this theatre of war, which was the true baptism of fire of the vehicle and made it universally known, saw the arrival of the T-26 brought by the Soviets to the friendly nation of Republican Spain. However, they were all sold in numbers of between 281 and 300 tanks. Together the Soviets added other vehicles such as the BT-5 and other armoured cars. Had it not been for the critical air inferiority, the Russian tank would have allowed the republicans to win the war given its superiority to the nationalist armoured vehicles. The Francoists, in turn, as the war progressed positively for them, ended up seizing numerous T-26 tanks and promptly reused them.
- Finnish Army: in the same way as the Spanish nationalists, the Finns, with a heroic and tactically well-positioned defence, managed first to destroy a large number of Russian tanks and finally to capture around 200 of them, which were immediately converted back into their armed forces and remained in force until the 1960s.
- German Army: during the initial phase of Operation Barbarossa, the Soviets lost thousands of T-26 tanks because had been hit, but most were abandoned on the spot due to the abrupt retreat that did not allow them to save all their weapons. The Germans did not reuse the Soviet tank, except for secondary roles such as artillery tractor and little else.
- Hungarian and Romanian armies: As mentioned in the previous paragraph, the Hungarian army, one of the most active of the German allies, also captured and obtained T-26s from the Germans, which were promptly put on staff.
- Republic of China: acquired 82 vehicles used by the Nationalist forces against the Japanese forces, and later used against the Chinese Communists in 1946-47.
- Turkey: 64 T-26s were purchased by the Turkish armed forces.

▲ Hungarian soldiers from the Eastern Front in front of the wreck of a T-26 tank. Péter Mujzer Archive.
▼ Soviet T-26 tank captured by Wehrmacht mounted units. By Bretho cc-by-sa-4-0.

XT FLAMETHROWER TANK, RUSSIA 1940

▲ HT Chemical Tanks (HT-26, HT-130, HT-133, HT-134), Russia 1940.

T-26 LIGHT TANK

TWE 49

▲ Hungarian soldiers from the Eastern Front have their photo taken in front of the wreckage of a late-model T-26 tank. Together with Germans, Finns and Romanians, the Hungarian army recovered many vehicles during the first phase of the invasion of the USSR. Péter Mujzer Archive.

▼ T-26 tank used by the Chinese army in Hunan in 1941.

T-26 A2 mod. 1938 new version with winter camouflage, Russia 1941.

T-26 A2 MOD. 1938 LIGHT TANK, RUSSIA 1941

DATA SHEET	
	T-26
Length	4550 mm
Width	2310 mm
Height	2300 mm
Track width	280 mm
Weight in combat order	9.600 kg
Crew	3 (commander/radio operator, driver, gunner)
Engine	4-cyl gas flat air-cooled Armstrong-Siddeley, 90 bhp
Maximum speed	31.16 km/h on-road and 19.3 km/h off-road
Autonomy	240 km on-road and 150 off-road
Suspension	Leaf spring with rocker arm
Armour thickness	6 to 15 mm
Armament	Early models: two DT (Degtjarëv) 7.62 machine gunsUltimate models: 47 mm gun and one DT 7.62
Production	10,300 examples

▼ Rear view of a T-26 Mod. 33 stored in a Russian park.

T-26 A2 MOD. 1938 LIGHT TANK, RUSSIA 1941

▲ T-26 A2 mod. 1938 new version with camouflage in tri-colour, Russia 1941.

▲ Damaged and trackless T-26 tank is observed by a Nationalist officer. Spain 1937.

◄ T-26 tanks occupy a large front area spring 1941, Russia.

▼ T-26 column approaching combat positions in Spain in 1937.

T-26 A2 MOD. 1939 LIGHT TANK, RUSSIA, AUTUMN 1941

▲ T-26 A2 mod. 1939 with number 6, Russia 1941.

TN 26 OBSERVATION WAGON, RUSSIA, LENINGRAD 1935

▲ TN 26 Workshop observation post Plant 185 named after Kirov, Leningrad 1935.

TR-1 TROOP CARRIER MOD. 1933, RUSSIA 1941

▲ TR-1 mod. 1933 Specifications: weight: 9.455 t - crew: 2 (tank leader and pilot) + 14 infantrymen

BIBLIOGRAPHY

- Michail Barjatinskij, *Lëgkij tank T-26. Modelist-Konstruktor.*, Moskva, Modelist-Konstruktor, 2003, p. 64.
- Mikhail Baryatinsky, *Light Tanks: T-27, T-38, BT, T-26, T-40, T-50, T-60, T-70*, Hersham, Surrey, Ian Allen, 2006, p. 96, ISBN 0-7110-3163-0.
- Michail Barjatinskij, *Sovetskie tanki v boju. Ot T-26 do IS-2*, Moskva, JAUZA, EKSMO, 2006, p. 352, ISBN 5-699-18740-5.
- Fernando Vallejo, *Profile guide Soviet war colors 1936-1945*. Interactive Madrid Spagna 2013
- Maksim Kolomiec e Michail Svirin, *T-26: mašiny na ego base*, Moskva, Strategija KM, 2003, p. 80, ISBN 5-901266-01-3.
- Maksim Kolomiec, *T-26. Tjažëlaja sud'ba lëgkogo tanka*, Moscow, Yauza, Strategiya KM, EKSMO, 2007, p. 128, ISBN 978-5-699-21871-4.
- Aleksandr Soljankin, Ivan Pavlov Ivan, Michail Pavlov e Igor' Želtov, *Otečestvennye bronirovannye mašiny. XX vek. Tom 1: 1905–1941*, Moskva, Exprint, 2002, p. 344, ISBN 5-94038-030-1.
- Michail Svirin e Maksim Kolomiec, *Legkij tank T-26 ARMADA No. 20*, Moskva, Exprint, 2000, p. 58, ISBN 5-94038-003-4.
- Zaloga, Steven J., Hnery Morsehead, *T-26 Light Tank Backbone of the Red Army* London, Osprey new Vanguard.
- Zaloga, Steven J., James Grandsen, *Soviet Tanks and Combat Vehicles of World War Two*, London, Arms and Armour Press, 1984 ISBN 0-85368-606-8.
- Janusz Ledwoch. *T-26 vol. 1, vol. 2 e vol. 3*. Wydawnictwo MILITARIA, Varsavia Polonia 2003.
- Appel, Erik; et al. (2001). Ekberg, Henrik (ed.). Finland i krig 1939–1940 – första delen (in Swedish). Espoo, Finland: Schildts förlag Ab. p. 261. ISBN 951-50-1182-5.
- Axworthy, Mark; Scafeș, Cornel; Crăciunoiu, Cristian [in Romanian] (1995). Third Axis Fourth Ally: Romanian Armed Forces in the European War, 1941-1945. London: Arms and Armour. ISBN 9781854092670.
- Baryatinskiy, Mikhail (2003). Legkiy Tank T-26 (Light Tank T-26) (in Russian). Moscow: Modelist-Konstruktor. Special Issue No. 2. Subscription index in the Rospechat Catalogue 73474.
- Baryatinskiy, Mikhail (2006). Light Tanks: T-27, T-38, BT, T-26, T-40, T-50, T-60, T-70. Hersham, Surrey: Ian Allan. ISBN 0-7110-3163-0.
- Baryatinskiy, Mikhail (2006a). Sovetskie tanki v boyu. Ot T-26 do IS-2 (Soviet tanks in action. From T-26 to IS-2) (in Russian). Moscow: YAUZA, EKSMO. ISBN 5-699-18740-5.
- Daley, John (1999). «Soviet and German Advisors Put Doctrine to the Test» in Armor, 1 May 1999. Fort Knox, KY: US Army Armor Center. ISSN 0004-2420.
- Franco, Lucas M. (2006). «El Tanque de la Guerra Civil Española». Historia de la Iberia Vieja (in Spanish). No. 13. ISSN 1699-7913.
- García, José María; Lucas Molina Franco (2005). La Brunete (in Spanish). Valladolid: Quiron Ediciones. p. 80. ISBN 84-96016-28-5.
- García, José María; Franco, Lucas Molina (2006). Las Armas de la Guerra Civil Española (in Spanish). Madrid: La Esfera de los Libros. p. 613. ISBN 84-9734-475-8.

BOOKS ALREADY PUBLISHED IN THE SERIES

TWE-017 EN

www.ingramcontent.com/pod-product-compliance
Lightning Source LLC
LaVergne TN
LVHW081539070526
838199LV00056B/3714